The Art of
Hand Shadows

Albert Almoznino

Photographs by Y. Pinas
Drawings by the Author

DOVER PUBLICATIONS, INC.
Mineola, New York

Bibliographical Note

This Dover edition, first published in 2001, is an unabridged republication
of the work originally published in 1970 by Stravon Educational Press, New
York.

Library of Congress Cataloging-in-Publication Data

Almoznino, Albert.
     The art of hand shadows / Albert Almoznino ; photographs by Y. Pinas,
drawings by the author.
         p. cm.
     Originally published: New York : Stravon Educational Press, c1970.
     ISBN 0-486-41876-6 (pbk.)
     1. Shadow-pictures. I. Pinas, Y., ill. II. Title.

GV1218.S5 A45 2001
791.5'8—dc21

                                                                2001047519

Manufactured in the United States of America
Dover Publications, Inc., 31 East 2nd Street, Mineola, N.Y. 11501

CONTENTS

6   CONTENTS

INTRODUCTION

The art of shadows, which probably originated in the Far East, was very popular in Europe in the 19th century, especially in France, where it was called *Ombres Chinoises*, meaning "Chinese shadows." Most of the shadowgraphers of the past were also magicians—for shadow art needs the same dexterity required by tricks of "magic."

In our day the art is declining because the electric lamp does not make good shadows. When the candle was a common source of illumination, shadows were sharply defined by night. People saw shadows of themselves on the wall and shadows of everything exposed by chance to the light of the candle.

In this book I would like to share with you my knowledge of the art of shadows. I hope you will benefit from my experience of years on the stage, and learn for yourself the pleasures of shadowgraphy.

THE TOOLS YOU NEED

YOUR HANDS
Exercise your hands to achieve elasticity.

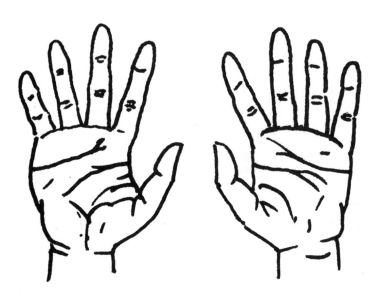

SOURCE OF LIGHT
The source of light may be a candle, a flashlight, or any small spot of light.

A SCREEN
A white sheet, a motion-picture
screen, or merely a bright wall
will serve the purpose.

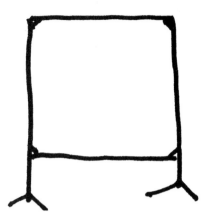

TECHNICAL INSTRUCTIONS

If you perform for a small audience at a party in a private home, you may project the shadows on a tablecloth or a sheet hung against the wall, or on a bare light-colored wall.

For a light source, you may use a candle or a flashlight. A candle gives a good dark shadow, a flashlight a stronger and more directional source; however, remove the reflector and glass of the flashlight, because they diffuse the shadow. An ordinary electric lamp may also be used, but the bulb must be unfrosted and very small, and you must be closer to the wall to obtain a good shadow.

Place the light in the middle of the room on a small table or tripod and sit between the light and the sheet or wall. You will see that the farther you go from the wall, the less sharp the shadow becomes. You must choose the correct distance so that the figures will be large and sharp. Now you are ready for the show.

If you perform on a stage, you need a screen, so that you can perform behind it and the audience sees only the shadows on the screen. The screen may be made of a sheet of muslin or other thin cloth attached to a frame.

In a nightclub, hall, or small theater, I like to use a portable nylon screen, four feet square, on a pliable aluminum frame. This type of screen is used sometimes for TV projection and is called a rear projection screen. With such a screen, however, the light must be stronger. Use a small spotlight without projector, lenses, or diffusors; or a motion-picture projector with the front lenses removed.

The best light source is a small arc lamp, because it gives a strong ray of bright light and projects very dark, sharp shadows. The only disadvantage is that you need a regulator for the current.

HOW TO PRODUCE SHADOWS

The first requirement for making live shadow pictures is to develop very flexible fingers. You can achieve this only by exercise. Begin with simple exercises and progress to more difficult ones.

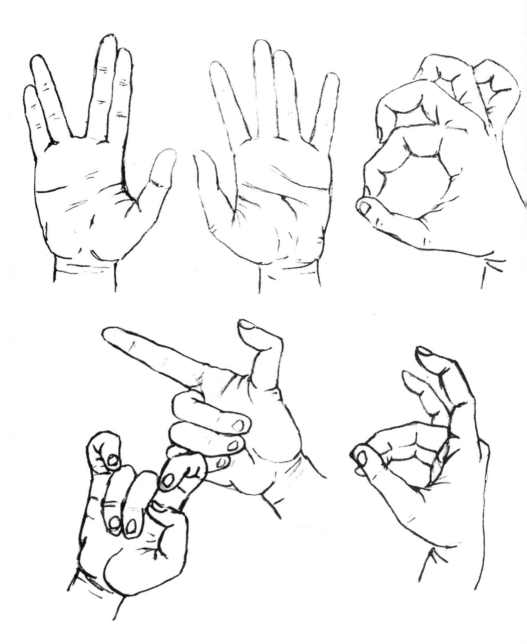

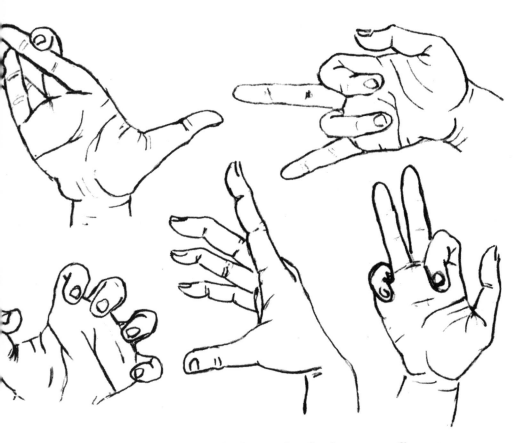

When you have full control of your hands, form one silhouette and practice it until you know it by heart; then go on to another one. When you have sufficient material for a show, organize it into a program. Make it as original and amusing as possible, and time it to take no more than twenty to twenty-five minutes.

The change from picture to picture should be quick, but give the audience time to see each silhouette and to enjoy it. Try to give motion and life to your figures.

Before each performance, make a list of your program, rehearse it, and learn it by heart. In this way, you will avoid having to improvise or make changes in the middle of the show. Also before each performance, check everything—the screen, the light, the position of your chair. Remember that you will be performing in the dark.

Musical accompaniment is very important. It makes the show more artistic and more interesting, and fills any unoccupied moments that may occur.

THE CRAB

The crab is easy to form by using both hands. It sidles quickly from side to side.

THE RABBIT

Make the rabbit as shown in the picture, with both hands. By moving the legs and the ears quickly, you can make the rabbit very lively.

THE RABBIT AND THE DOG

Leave the head and ears of the rabbit on the screen and with the other hand make a dog, which attacks and swallows the rabbit.

THE JACKAL

The jackal is an evil-looking animal that is easily turned into a wolf, as shown in the next shadow.

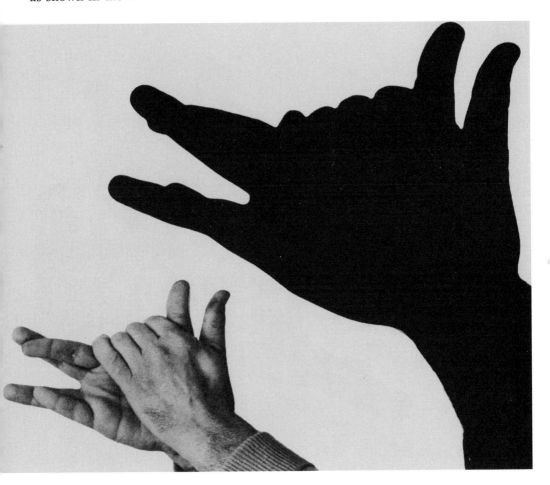

THE WOLF

If the position of the hands is just right, you will form a very realistic eye. The eye can be made to move by moving just the finger.

If you can imitate the howling of the animal and synchronize the sound and the movements, you will obtain a very good effect.

THE HORSE

The horse can be made to neigh by separating the fingers that form its muzzle.

THE DONKEY

The donkey can be made to wiggle his ears and bray.

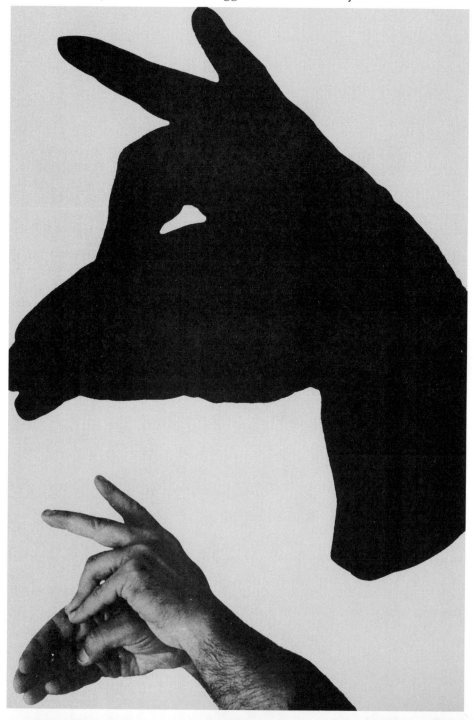

THE CAMEL

The camel should move very slowly, like a real "ship of the desert."

THE ELEPHANT

To give life to the character move the trunk, sometimes upward and sometimes back toward the mouth, as in the second picture.

THE KANGAROO

The kangaroo looks as if it might have a young one in its pouch.

THE DEER

This antlered animal is majestic. He moves his head up and down.

THE FAWN

All children are fond of the little fawn who moves his eye and wags his tail. In the second picture, when the tail refuses to stop wagging, the fawn becomes angry—and nips at the tail!

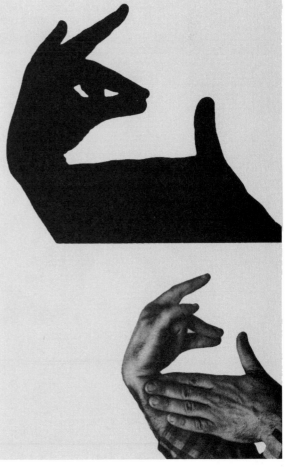

THE DUCK

I imitate his voice. He rolls his eye and sticks out his tongue.

THE SWAN

This graceful animal easily turns its neck in all directions, drinks from the lake, and stretches its wings. Emphasize its elegant movements, as shown in the three pictures.

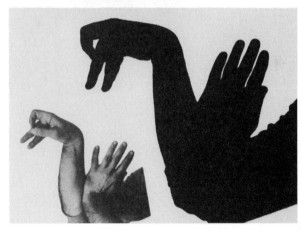

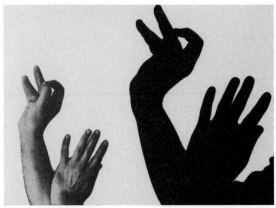

THE ROOSTING HEN

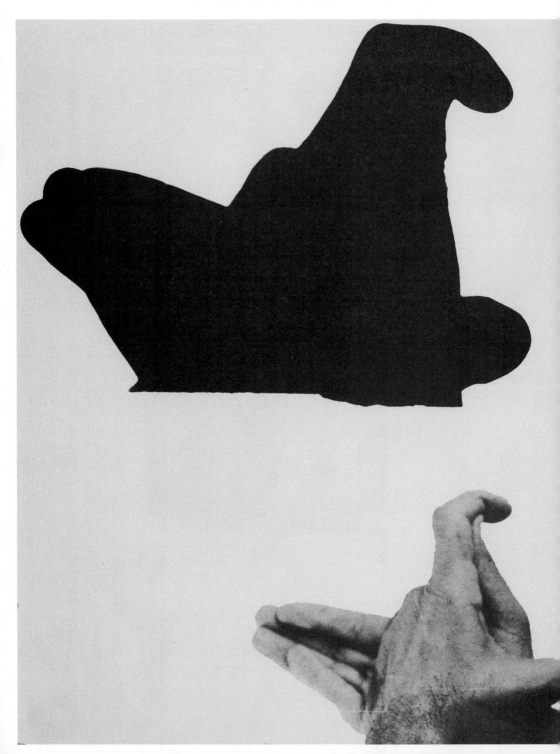

THE PEACOCK

This stately bird walks slowly and waves its long tail.

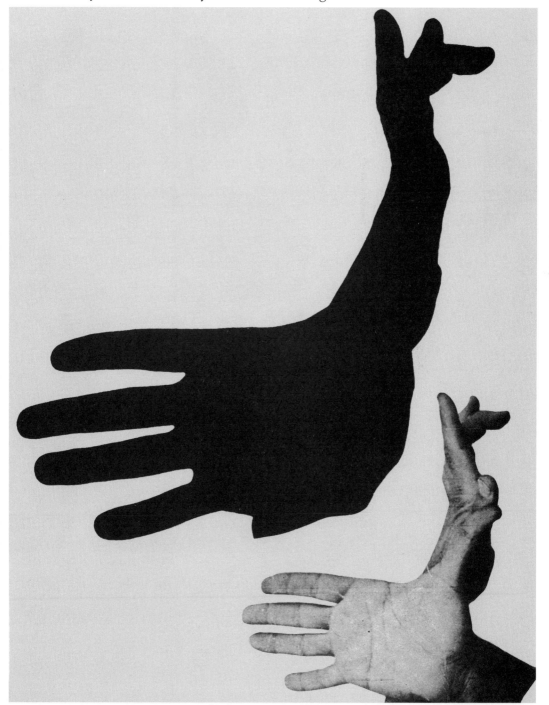

THE COW

The cow can be made to lower its head and moo.

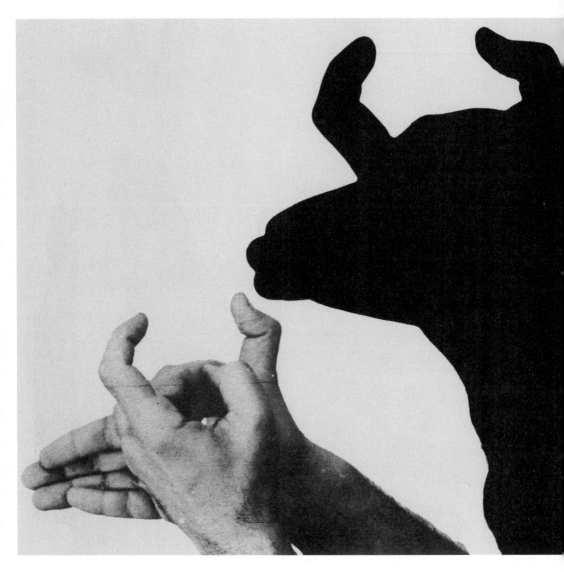

THE GIRAFFE AND THE MONKEY

The monkey scratches the neck of the giraffe.

TWO MONKEYS

Two monkeys facing each other can make many entertaining gestures.

THE DINOSAUR

The angry-looking dinosaur almost makes us glad he is extinct.

THE EAGLE

The close-up of the eagle's head shows its strong beak. In the second picture the great bird stands majestically on a branch and turns its head slowly. In the third and fourth pictures it flies slowly toward the audience and becomes larger and larger until it covers the entire screen.

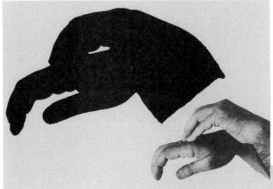

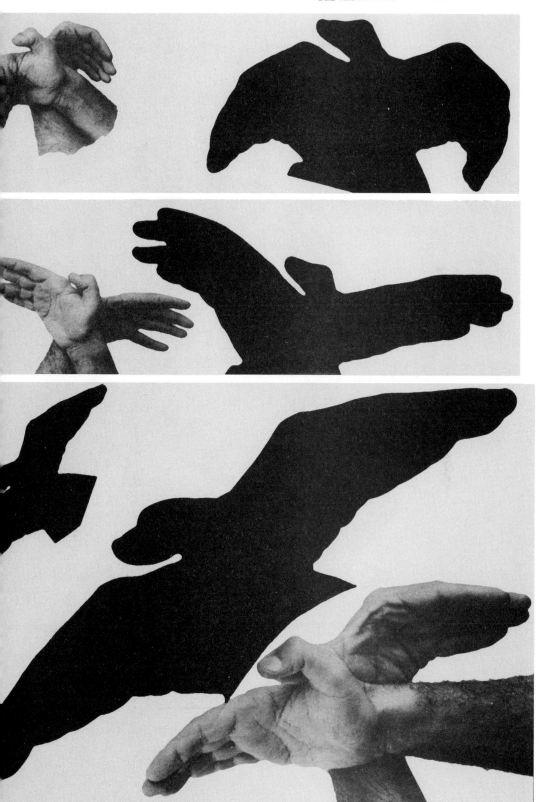

THE PANTHER

The snarling panther seems ready to spring at its prey.

THE CAT

The cat takes many positions. In the first picture it is sitting tidily. Then it scratches itself, lashes its tail, and jumps toward the audience. It may become bigger and bigger, and finally leave only its tail on the screen.

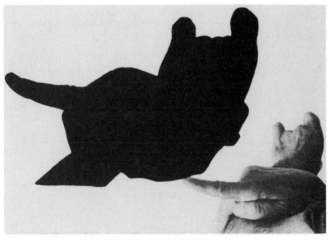

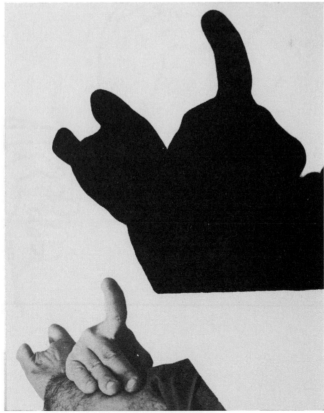

PEOPLE

The human face is always shown in profile. It is made by using both hands.

One hand forms the face and other forms the forehead and head.

A little space left between the two hands gives the appearance of an eye.

Using these principles, you can form many types by changing the position of the fingers.

Later, when you have experience in making shadows, you can create the likenesses of famous personalities. Always choose people with a strong characteristic profile.

In the following pages you will see various types of heads.

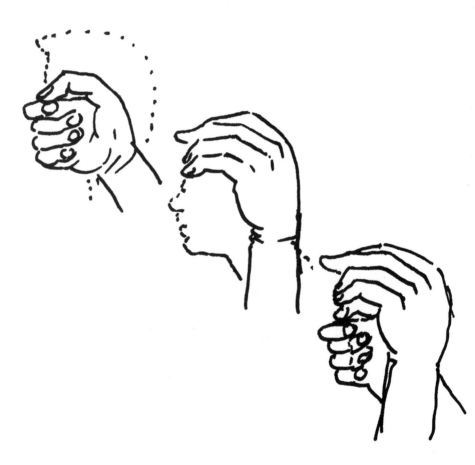

THE AMERICAN INDIAN

The Indian wears a characteristic feathered headdress.

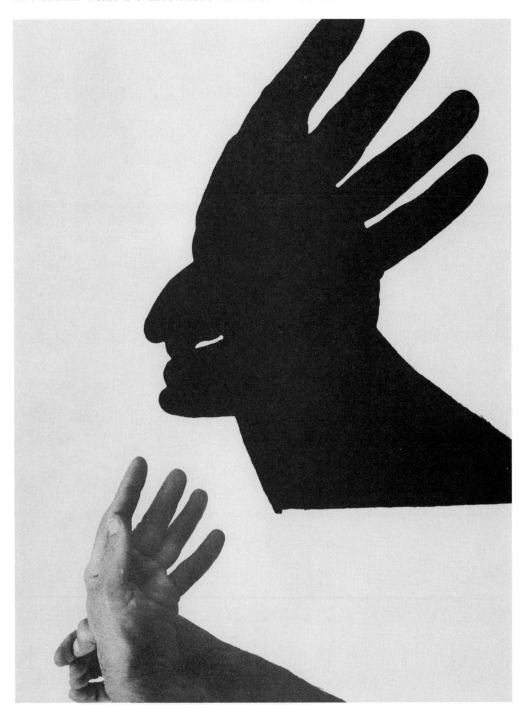

VATICAN PRELATES

Roman Catholic prelates can sometimes be recognized by their traditional headgear.

BASEBALL PLAYER

The typical brimmed cap shades the eyes of the outfielder.

FARMER

The farmer wears a shapeless old hat as he goes about his chores.

COWBOY

The cowboy is known by his traditional ten-gallon hat.

ABRAHAM LINCOLN

The "Great Emancipator" had an unmistakable profile.

STALIN

The Russian dictator's heavy moustache comes through clearly in shadow art.

JOHN F. KENNEDY

The strong features of the youthful President are easy to reproduce in shadow.

DE GAULLE

The hero of the French Resistance is recognizable by his large nose and his French army cap.

BEN-GURION

The former Israeli prime minister is easily identified by his bushy "halo" of hair.

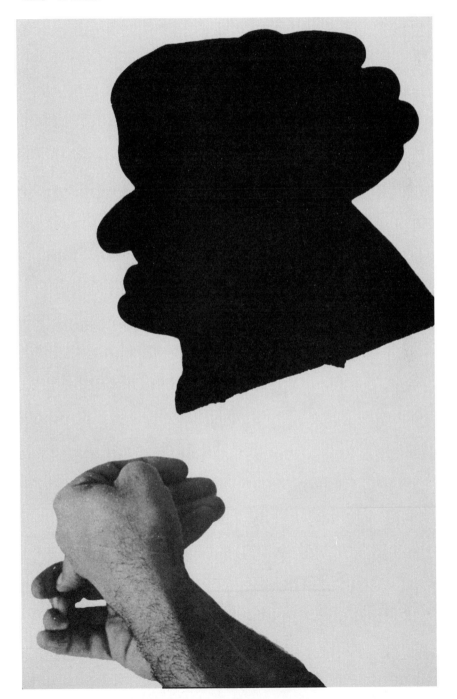

RICHARD M. NIXON

The 37th President of the United States is quickly recognizable by his sloping nose and large forehead.

GAMAL ABDEL NASSER

The Egyptian president has an unmistakable nose and jaw.

FIDEL CASTRO

The Cuban revolutionary leader and premier is recognizable by his beard and his favorite military fatigue cap.

PLANTS AND FLOWERS
OF THE DESERT

The plants move onto the screen from one side, remain a moment, then continue across to disappear at the other side of the screen.
    Some figures change from one form to another.

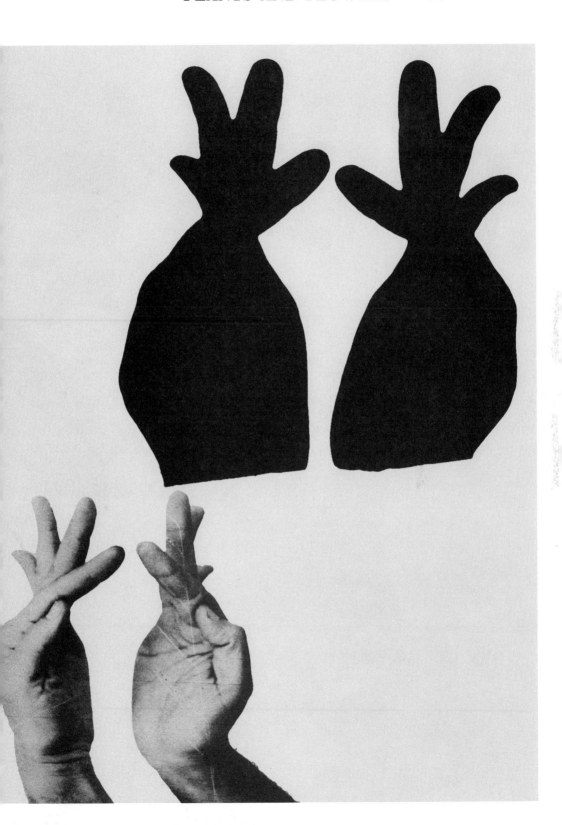

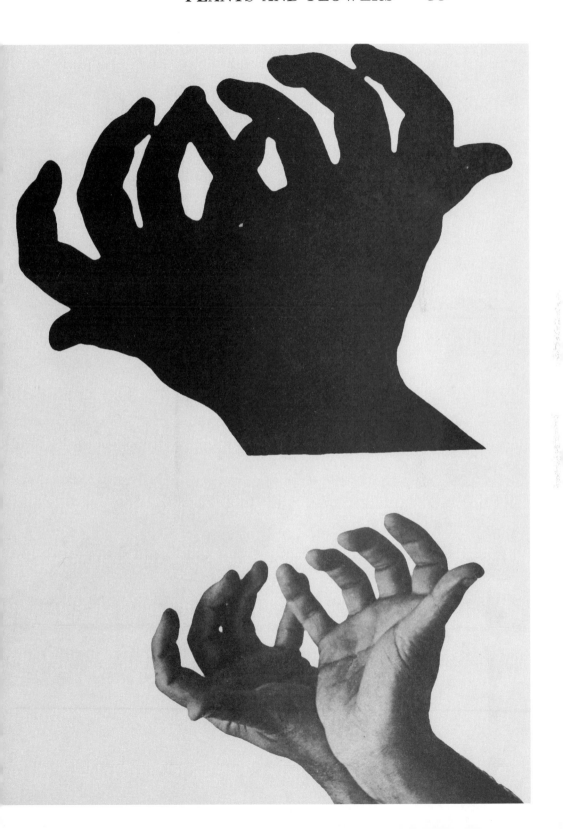

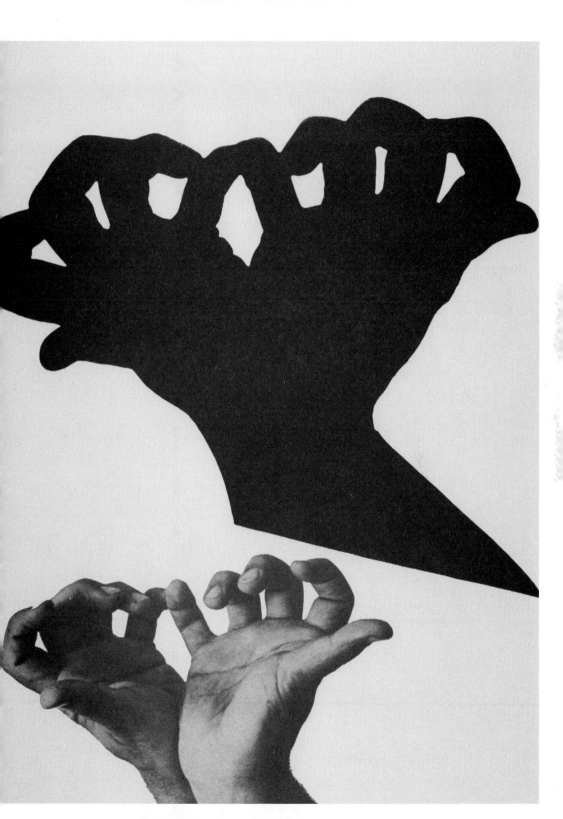

EIFFEL TOWER

A match contributes a special effect to the famous Paris landmark.

CHURCHES

Houses of worship are built in many styles. Here are shadows of two types of churches.

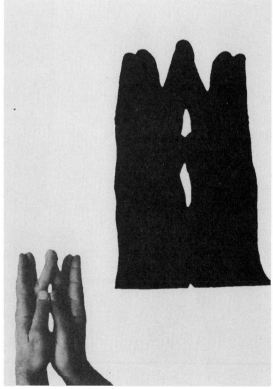

TOWER

PAGODA

CONCLUSION

People all over the world love to form shadows, and almost everyone has tried at one time or another to project shadows of a dog or a horse on a bright wall.

The art is inexpensive, is performed without the use of language, and appeals especially to children, regardless of nationality or age. It stimulates and sharpens the imagination by giving life to forms and animals from nature.

Of course, the pictures in this book are motionless. But the hands and the fingers are dynamic and can give movement to the shadows. Add some distinctive motions and gestures to give life and character to the silhouette.

With appropriate background music, a shadowgraph show will give joy and amusement to everyone.